SRA Open Court Reading

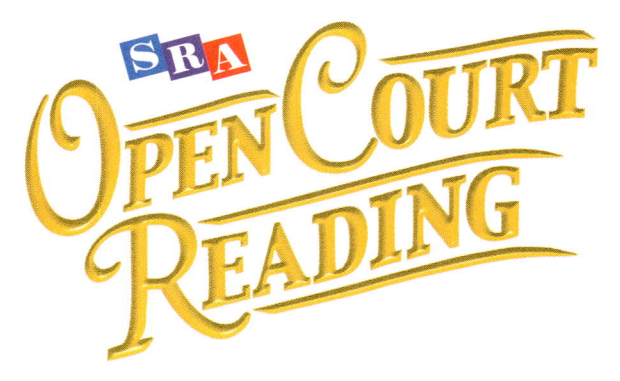

Rose Takes a Hike

SRA
A Division of The McGraw-Hill Companies
Columbus, Ohio

www.sra4kids.com

SRA/McGraw-Hill
A Division of The **McGraw·Hill** Companies

Copyright © 2002 by SRA/McGraw-Hill.

All rights reserved. Except as permitted under the United States Copyright Act, no part of this publication may be reproduced or distributed in any form or by any means, or stored in a database or retrieval system, without prior written permission from the publisher.

Printed in the United States of America.

Send all inquiries to:
SRA/McGraw-Hill
8787 Orion Place
Columbus, OH 43240-4027

ISBN 0-07-569730-0
3 4 5 6 7 8 9 DBH 05 04 03 02

Mike and Jane like riding bikes and hiking for exercise.

Jane has a dog. Her name is Rose.
Rose likes hiking with them in the park.

Jane and Mike hold a rope and climb rocks. Rose slides off.

Racing bikes makes them tired.
Mike and Jane doze in the shade.

Rose rolls in a nice place.
She is poking her nose in a hole.

A spider runs from the hole.
Rose goes after the spider.

Rose hikes past some wild mice.
Rose is tasting a pine cone.

Don't go in the cold lake, Rose!
Splash!

Rose hikes more.
Rose is lost, and she whines.

Later, Mike and Jane wake up.
Jane tells Mike, "Rose is missing!
I hope I am able to find her."

"I will help," says Mike.
Mike and Jane ride for a while.

At the lake, Mike finds wet dog prints.
Jane finds Rose under a pile of crates!

"Rose is safe!" yells Jane.
"Let's go home."

Jane makes space for Rose.
Rose thinks a ride is nice
after such a long hike.